THE LEADERSHIP FAIRWAY

Parallels Between Golf and
Exceptional Leadership

WAYNE E. SMITH

Copyright © 2025, Wayne E. Smith

All rights reserved. No part of this book may be used or reproduced by any means, graphic, electronic, or mechanical (including any information storage retrieval system) without the express written permission from the author, except in the case of brief quotations for use in articles and reviews wherein appropriate attribution of the source is made.

ISBN: 978-1-965937-10-5 (Hardcover)
ISBN: 978-1-965937-09-9 (Paperback)
ISBN: 978-1-965937-11-2 (ePub)

Because of the dynamic nature of the Internet, web addresses or links contained in this book may have been changed since publication and may no longer be valid. The content of this book and all expressed opinions are those of the author and do not reflect the publisher or the publishing team. The author is solely responsible for all content included herein.

Cover design by Eswari Kamireddy
Edited by Eswari Kamireddy
Interior design by Eswari Kamireddy

I dedicate this book to my brother-in-law, Dennis Brown, whose decades-long career as a fireman, his dedication to the game of golf, and in all aspects of his life encapsulate the pinnacle of integrity, humility, and courage.

"Golf teaches you lessons about patience, perseverance, and integrity—the very principles that shape a meaningful life."

— **Tom Watson.**

Contents

Preface ix

1. Tee Off with Integrity – The Foundation of Leadership 1
2. The Power of Focus – Staying the Course in Leadership 5
3. Course Management – Strategic Thinking in Leadership 11
4. The Drive for Success – Motivation and Leadership 19
5. Mastering the Short Game – Attention to Detail in Leadership ... 27
6. The Importance of Practice – Continuous Improvement in Leadership ... 35
7. Handling Hazards – Overcoming Obstacles in Leadership ... 43
8. Playing with Patience – The Role of Patience in Leadership ... 51
9. The Ethics of the Game – Leading with Fairness and Respect ... 59
10. Finishing Strong – Leaving a Lasting Leadership Legacy ... 67

Epilogue: The Leadership Fairway: A Continuous Journey 75
Conclusion 83
Afterward 85
Teeing Up Success: Further Leadership Lessons from Golf 89

Preface

There is much to be admired about golf. The serenity of the fairways, the precision of a well-struck shot, and the camaraderie shared among players all hold a certain allure. However, despite my appreciation for the sport, I discovered early on, as a college student, that my poor hand-eye coordination, plus being left-handed, presented specific challenges. This made mastering the game too complicated for my willingness to endure frustratingly.

Much later in life, however, I found a different path that allowed me to immerse myself in golf without perfecting my swing. After retiring as an advertising executive in Los Angeles, and for over a decade, I produced television golf programs in the Palm Springs area of Southern California, a region known for its breathtaking courses and as a hub for both the PGA and Senior PGA Tours. My work brought me into close contact with some of the greatest golfers of our time, allowing me to observe the game from tee box to green and from a unique vantage point.

During this time, one of my most profound experiences was working closely with Tommy Jacobs, a celebrated PGA and Senior PGA Tour player. Tommy was an exceptional golfer and a man of deep integrity, humility, and kindness. His approach to the game—rooted in respect for the sport, unwavering focus, and an innate sense of fair play—left a lasting impression on me. Through Tommy, I saw how golf was more than just a competition; it reflected life's fundamental principles.

Producing these golf programs offered me a front-row seat to witness the parallels between golf and life. I spent countless hours on some of the most beautiful courses in the world, capturing the fairways' ambiance, the players' concentration, and the game's elegance. But what struck me most was how the tenets of golf—integrity, patience, resilience, and strategic thinking—mirrored exceptional leadership qualities. I observed that golf wasn't just a sport; it was a teacher offering lessons far beyond the green.

In *The Leadership Fairway*, I draw from my experiences behind the camera, working alongside legends like Tommy Jacobs, to explore the rich parallels between golf and leadership. This book is not just for golfers or leaders but anyone who strives to live with purpose, integrity, and a commitment to continuous improvement. Each chapter delves into a different aspect of the game and how it relates to leadership, offering insights and lessons that can be applied on and off the course.

As I guide you through these pages, I hope you will see the beauty in golf and leadership as continuous journeys that require dedication, reflection, and an unwavering commitment to excellence. Whether you're leading a team or simply navigating life, the principles of golf can offer profound guidance.

I may not have mastered the game of golf with my hands, but through the lens of my camera and the wisdom of those I worked with, I've come to understand its deeper meanings. I invite you to walk this fairway with me, explore golf lessons, and apply them to your leadership journey.

NOTE: *As a non-golfer I am unfamiliar with many of golf's unique terminology, so I researched and sought AI's assistance to write in the game's vernacular.*

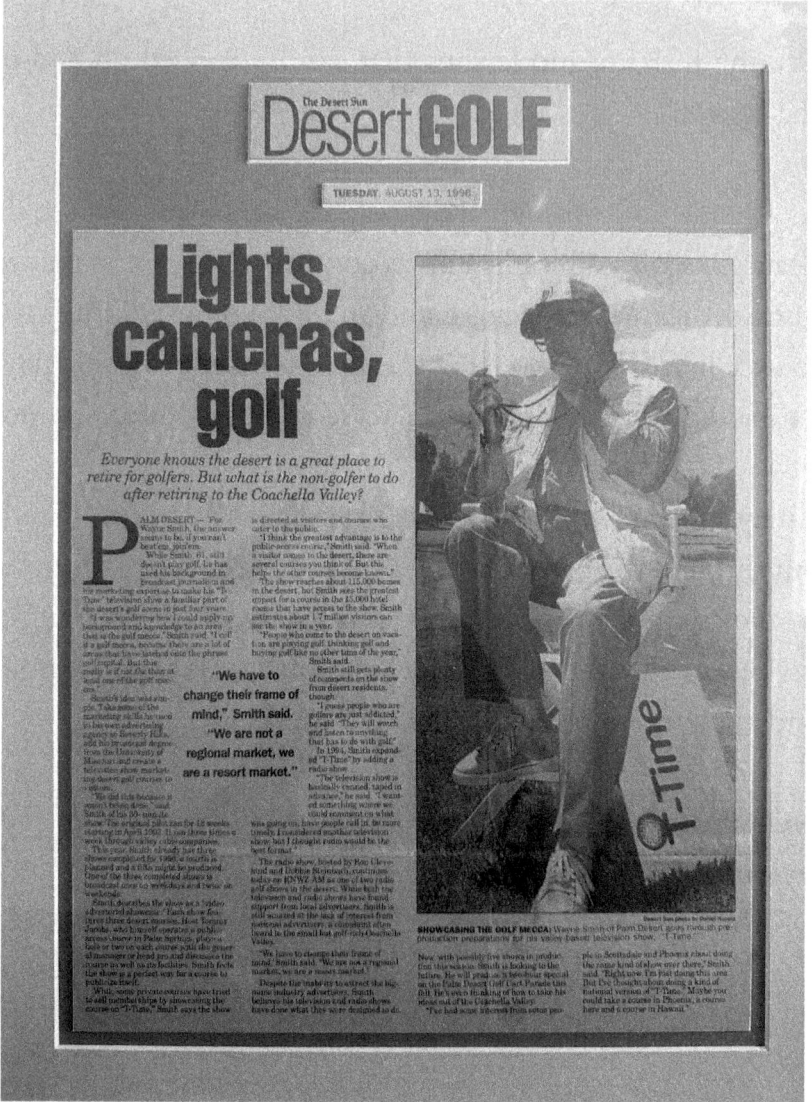

Pictured here is the author, Wayne E. Smith, on a Palm Springs-area golf course, directing the videotaping of a scene for the popular golf television program T-Time with host the late PGA Tour player Tommy Jacobs. Smith created, produced, and directed the programs that aired daily in the Palm Springs area for over a decade in the late 1990s and early 2000s.

1

Tee Off with Integrity – The Foundation of Leadership

A Sport Built on Honor

Picture this: You're standing on the 18th green, just a putt away from victory. There are no referees, no instant replays, just you and the honor of the game. You notice your ball moved slightly, perhaps because of the wind or an accidental nudge. No one saw it, and you could easily ignore it. But true golfers don't. They call the penalty on themselves.

Golf, unlike many sports, is built on self-regulation. No officials are watching every move. Instead, golfers must hold themselves accountable to the rules, even when no one else is watching. This unwritten code of honesty and integrity makes golf more than just a game—it reflects character. In many ways, it mirrors the essence of outstanding leadership.

Integrity: The Core of Leadership

Integrity isn't about making the easy choice—it's about making the right choice. Just as a golfer must play by the rules, leaders must uphold ethical standards, even when the path is difficult.

The best leaders—whether in the boardroom, on the golf course, or leading a nation—understand that trust is their most valuable currency. It's built one decision at a time. They don't take shortcuts, bend the rules for convenience, or compromise their values under pressure. Like a golfer who plays an honest round, great leaders consistently lead, earning respect through their actions, not just words.

Leading by Example

Professionals calling a penalty on themselves in golf sets a powerful example for others. Jack Nicklaus, one of the greatest golfers ever, never compromised his integrity, even in the most competitive moments. He knew that character was more important than trophies.

Leaders operate the same way. Their team watches their every move. If a leader cuts corners, their employees will do the same. But when leaders hold themselves to the highest ethical standard—owning their mistakes, staying accountable, and making decisions with integrity—it fosters a culture of honesty and trust.

The True Test of Character

Integrity isn't tested when things are easy—it's tested when the stakes are high. There are moments of temptation in golf: a slight rule infraction that no one would notice, a questionable drop that could gain an advantage. The same moments exist in leadership—choosing between a quick win or doing the right thing, even if it costs you.

The objective measure of a leader is how they act when no one is watching. Do they stay true to their values when under pressure? Do they make decisions based on principles, not popularity? Just as a golfer's true character is revealed on the course, a leader's legacy is defined by their commitment to integrity.

The Long Game: Building a Legacy of Trust

The success that comes from dishonesty is fleeting. A golfer who cheats may win a tournament, but they'll lose the respect of their peers. A leader who lacks integrity may rise quickly, but their influence won't last.

In golf and leadership, the greats understand that integrity is the foundation of lasting success. People trust them, believe in them, and follow them not because they're perfect but because they're honest.

Warren Buffett built one of the most successful companies in the world by always putting integrity first. Indra Nooyi led PepsiCo with a commitment to transparency and ethical leadership. Nelson Mandela's moral compass shaped history. These leaders didn't just succeed—they left a legacy of trust, proving that leadership, like golf, is a game of honor.

Teeing Off with Integrity

Golf teaches us that the best rounds aren't just about skill—they're about character. Leadership is the same. Whether you're making decisions for a team, a company, or a nation, your integrity will define your success.

So the next time you step onto the course—or into a leadership role—remember this: The most important thing you can bring isn't just talent or ambition. It's integrity. Because in the end, it's not just about how well you play the game—it's about how honorably you play it.

2

The Power of Focus – Staying the Course in Leadership

A Game of Concentration

Imagine you're on the 16th hole of a championship match. The crowd is silent, the wind barely rustles the trees, and a single putt stands between you and victory. But the green slopes subtly, the pressure mounts, and distractions threaten to creep in. Stay focused. Stay in the moment. Execute.

Golf is as much a mental game as it is a physical one. A lapse in concentration—even for a second—can derail an entire round. The best golfers know that success isn't just about skill but focus, discipline, and the ability to block distractions.

Leadership is no different. The world around a leader is filled with competing priorities, unexpected challenges, and the constant pull of distractions. The ability to maintain a laser-sharp focus on long-term goals while managing the immediate obstacles separates genuinely great leaders from the rest.

Focus in Golf: The Art of Being Present

In golf, every shot requires complete attention. The past doesn't matter—the bogey from the last hole is behind you. The future is uncertain—the next hole will come soon enough. What matters is the shot in front of you.

This ability to be fully present is what makes a golfer great. Players like Tiger Woods and Jack Nicklaus were known for their talent, unshakable concentration, ability to block out distractions, and commitment to each shot.

But golf isn't just about executing one shot—it's about playing the entire course. Every golfer must balance short-term focus with long-term strategy, making decisions that serve their overall game plan. Do they take a risk with an aggressive shot or play it safe? Do they adapt to the shifting wind or stick to their original approach?

This balancing act between the present moment and the long game is the essence of effective leadership.

Focus in Leadership: Balancing Vision and Execution

Great leaders, like great golfers, know where they're going. They have a clear vision of their goals and what they want to achieve. But having a vision isn't enough—it must be paired with the discipline to stay focused, avoid distractions, and make intentional decisions that align with long-term success.

Long-Term Vision: Leaders, like golfers, must have an end goal in mind. Whether building a company, transforming an industry, or creating lasting change, success is built on a clear and compelling vision.

Managing Short-Term Challenges: Just as a golfer focuses on one shot at a time, a leader must handle daily challenges without losing sight of the bigger picture. The best leaders pivot when necessary but never abandon their mission.

Leaders who get too caught up in short-term fires lose sight of their broader goals. When they focus only on the big picture, they neglect the critical daily decisions that bring it to life. Authentic leadership requires shifting focus between the present and the future—just as a golfer shifts between individual shots and overall strategy.

The Mental Game: Staying Composed Under Pressure

Focus isn't just about looking ahead—it's about staying mentally strong, even when the stakes are high.

In golf, the pressure of competition can rattle even the best players. A missed putt, a bad lie, or a sudden shift in weather can throw off an entire game. But the most significant players don't dwell on mistakes. They reset, refocus, and move forward.

Leadership is filled with similar moments—unexpected crises, tough decisions, and external pressures that test a leader's mental resilience. The ability to stay calm, think clearly, and focus under pressure sets extraordinary leaders apart.

The best leaders and the best golfers share a common trait: they don't let the moment overwhelm them. They train their minds to stay composed, trust their preparation, and confidently execute.

The Long Game: Discipline and Consistency

Success in both golf and leadership isn't built overnight. It's the product of consistent effort, discipline, and commitment to improvement.

Golfers spend years refining their swings, studying courses, and training their minds to handle high-stakes moments. They know that one great shot doesn't make a champion—but years of great habits do.

Leadership works the same way. The most effective leaders don't let distractions distract them from their mission. They wake up daily and take intentional steps toward their vision, even when progress feels slow.

Leaders who remain consistent in their values, decisions, and work ethic build trust and credibility, leading to lasting success.

Tuning Out the Noise

Every leader, like every golfer, must learn to block out distractions. In golf, the crowd, the leaderboard, the wind, and even self-doubt can cloud a player's focus. However, the greats develop techniques to tune out the noise and focus on the task.

For leaders, the noise comes in different forms—outside opinions, short-term setbacks, competing priorities, and constant demands. But the best leaders, like the best golfers, learn to filter out what truly matters from what is merely a distraction.

Staying the Course

At the heart of golf and leadership is a simple but profound truth: success belongs to those who can focus on the right things at the right time for the right reasons.

A golfer who lets frustration take over loses their rhythm. A leader who chases too many distractions loses their purpose.

But the ones who stay focused, keep their eyes on the long-term goal, and commit to the process day after day? They are the ones who achieve greatness.

Whether standing over a putt on the 18th green or making a tough leadership decision, the lesson is the same: Tune out the noise, trust your vision, and focus on what matters.

The rest will take care of itself.

3

Course Management – Strategic Thinking in Leadership

The Golfer's Dilemma: Play It Safe or Take the Risk?

Picture yourself on the 15th hole of a championship golf course. It's a long par 5, the fairway winding through a sea of bunkers, with water guarding the green. You have a choice: take a safe layup, positioning yourself for a straightforward third shot, or **go for it**, trying to land on the green in two, risking a disaster if your shot veers off course.

What's the right decision?

The best golfers don't leave that choice to chance. They study the course, anticipate challenges, and make strategic decisions that position them for success.

The same is true in leadership. Leaders face constant decision points, each with its risks and rewards. Like a great golfer, a great leader knows that strategy is everything—not just making decisions at the moment but thinking ahead, adjusting to obstacles, and keeping the big picture in mind.

Both golf and leadership require strategic thinking—the ability to analyze the terrain, anticipate challenges, and make calculated moves that align with the long-term vision.

Course Management in Golf: Thinking Several Shots Ahead

Success in golf isn't just about executing the perfect swing—it's about understanding the course and playing it smart.

Understanding the Course: A golfer who masters a course knows every detail—the greens' slope, the bunkers' depth, the way the wind shifts on different holes. They don't just step up and swing; they plan every shot based on knowledge and foresight.

Anticipating Challenges: No golfer expects a smooth round. There will be wind gusts, bad lies, tricky pin placements, and pressure-packed moments. The best players anticipate these challenges and adjust their strategy accordingly, ensuring they don't let one mistake derail their entire game.

This same level of careful preparation and adaptability defines the best leaders. Leaders who fail to analyze their landscape or anticipate potential roadblocks find themselves reacting instead of leading.

Great leaders, like great golfers, don't just hope for the best—they prepare for any scenario.

Strategic Thinking in Leadership: Navigating the Terrain

Just as golfers need to understand the course, leaders must understand the business environment in which they operate. The most successful leaders don't react to events—they anticipate them.

Understanding the Environment: Every organization operates within a landscape of trends, competitors, and shifting challenges. Leaders must analyze these factors just as a golfer studies the layout of a course before playing a round.

Anticipating Obstacles: Change is inevitable. Markets shift, competitors evolve, and crises emerge. The best leaders don't wait for challenges to appear—they prepare for them in advance.

Just as a golfer walks onto the course with a game plan,

leaders must guide their teams with clarity and purpose, ensuring every move supports the overall vision.

The Balance Between Strategy and Adaptability

Even the best golfers and the best leaders face unexpected situations. A golfer may plan for one strategy, only to realize mid-round that conditions demand a change in approach.

Planning and Adaptability: A solid plan is essential, as is the ability to adapt when unexpected. A golfer who insists on sticking to their original strategy—despite changing weather conditions—sets themselves up for failure. A leader who clings to an outdated plan, ignoring new realities, faces the same fate.

Risk Management: Strategic thinking involves knowing when to be aggressive and when to play it safe. A golfer must decide whether to attack the pin or lay up, and a leader must choose when to take bold risks and when to proceed cautiously.

Like the best golfers, leaders don't make reckless choices—they make smart, calculated ones.

Playing the Long Game: Aligning Daily Decisions with the Ultimate Goal

A golfer doesn't win a tournament by focusing only on one hole at a time—they strategize for the full 18 holes.

A leader, too, must balance immediate actions with long-term goals.

Creating a Roadmap: Every golfer approaches a course with a clear plan, mapping out their approach to each hole. Leaders must do the same—defining a vision, setting milestones, and ensuring that every decision moves the organization forward.

Communicating the Strategy: A golfer has a caddy to help guide their decisions, but the entire team needs to be aligned in leadership. Leaders must clearly articulate the vision and ensure that every team member understands their role in achieving success.

When leaders consistently align their decisions with their long-term vision, they build momentum and consistency, just like a golfer working toward a winning round.

Lessons from the Great Strategic Thinkers

The world's most significant leaders have one thing in common: They didn't just react to the present—they shaped the future through strategic vision.

Jeff Bezos (Amazon): From selling books online to building a global tech empire, Bezos led Amazon through a series of strategic expansions, always thinking three steps ahead.

Angela Merkel (Former Chancellor of Germany): Merkel's ability to navigate political and economic crises with calm, calculated decision-making solidified her reputation as one of the most effective leaders of her time.

Howard Schultz (Starbucks): Schultz didn't just grow Starbucks—he built a global brand by anticipating market trends and ensuring every move aligned with the company's long-term success.

Like a great golfer, these leaders studied their environment, anticipated challenges, and made bold yet calculated decisions that led to lasting success.

Strategic Thinking Under Pressure

A golfer doesn't panic when they hit a bad shot. They analyze their position, adjust their plan, and make the most brilliant move possible given the circumstances.

A leader's job is no different. In times of crisis or uncertainty, the best leaders don't freeze up or make rash decisions. They stay composed, assess their options, and make choices that align with their strategy.

Scenario Planning: The best golfers practice shots for every situation—from tricky bunker shots to high-pressure putts—so nothing catches them off guard. Leaders must prepare similarly, thinking through possible challenges and developing solutions.

Risk Management: Every decision carries a level of risk. Do you take a bold move or play conservatively? The best leaders weigh the risks and rewards, ensuring their choices align with long-term objectives.

In golf and leadership, those who can stay calm, think ahead, and execute with confidence are the ones who rise to the top.

Managing the Course to Victory

A championship golfer doesn't just play—they strategize, adapt, and execute with precision.

A great leader does the same. By developing strategic thinking, staying adaptable, and ensuring every decision aligns with a long-term vision, leaders can guide their organizations to success—just as the best golfers navigate their way to victory.

So the next time you step onto the tee—or into a leadership role—take a deep breath, study the landscape, and make your move with strategy, confidence, and purpose.

The course is yours to manage.

4

The Drive for Success – Motivation and Leadership

The Power Behind the First Swing

You step up to the tee. The fairway stretches ahead, wide and inviting, yet filled with potential hazards. A strong, well-placed drive could set you up for a birdie. A poor one might force you to scramble to save par. In this moment, it's not just about power but precision, confidence, and vision.

A golfer's drive is more than just the opening shot—it's the foundation for the hole ahead. It sets the Tone, dictates the strategy, and builds momentum for the rest of the round. Similarly, a leader's drive—fueled by motivation and ambition—propels an organization forward. Just as a golfer harnesses focus, strength, and technique to execute a perfect drive, leaders must channel their determination, clarity, and energy to guide their team toward success.

The best golfers don't just swing hard and hope—they prepare, visualize, and execute purposefully. The best leaders do the same.

The Drive-in Golf: Power with Purpose

A powerful drive can differ between a smooth approach to the green or a struggle to recover. But power alone isn't enough—accuracy, control, and mental preparation are equally important.

Power and Precision: The most significant drivers of the ball—legends like Tiger Woods, Jack Nicklaus, and Rory McIlroy—combine raw power with deliberate precision. They don't just swing hard; they align their stance, grip, and body movement to achieve maximum efficiency and control.

Focus on the Target: Before taking the shot, a golfer must envision the path—picking a specific target, adjusting for conditions, and ensuring that every motion contributes to the intended outcome.

This is precisely what great leaders do. They don't just "go big" with ambition; they align their energy, strategy, and team efforts toward a clear goal. A leader's ability to set a strong direction, communicate a compelling vision, and maintain laser-sharp focus ensures that their organization stays on course.

Leadership Drive: Fueling Motivation and Ambition

Leaders, like golfers, must rely on internal motivation to push forward—especially when challenges arise. Their drive isn't just about their success; it's about inspiring their teams, setting the Tone, and creating momentum that carries the organization forward.

Channeling Inner Drive: Just as a golfer transfers energy into the swing, leaders must tap into their inner ambition—a deep, personal motivation that fuels passion, determination, and resilience.

Setting the Tone for the Team: A strong drive isn't just an individual achievement—it creates momentum that affects the entire team. When leaders demonstrate enthusiasm, commitment, and relentless pursuit of excellence, their team mirrors that energy.

Much like how a well-executed drive can boost confidence for the rest of the round, a leader's ambition creates an environment where teams feel empowered to perform at their highest level.

The Resilience Factor: Overcoming Challenges

Not every drive lands perfectly in the fairway. Even the best golfers find themselves in tough spots—deep rough, fairway bunkers, or tricky angles. But what separates champions from average players is how they recover.

Resilience and Perseverance: A lousy drive doesn't mean the hole is lost—it's the next shot that matters most. The same is true in leadership. Setbacks don't define a leader; their response to them does.

Continuous Improvement: No golfer masters their drive overnight. Even elite players analyze their swing, refine their technique, and seek constant improvement. Similarly, great leaders never stop learning, adjusting, and growing. They seek feedback, refine their skills, and adapt to new challenges with a lifelong growth mindset.

The best leaders and golfers embrace setbacks as opportunities to improve rather than reasons to retreat.

Leading by Example: Inspiring the Team to Follow

A well-struck drive is exhilarating—it sets the stage for a great round. But it also inspires those watching. Fans admire a golfer who confidently steps up and delivers, and teams admire a leader who does the same.

Leading by Example: When a leader demonstrates dedication, discipline, and passion, it naturally inspires others to rise. Employees don't just follow words—they follow actions.

Creating a Vision of Success: An incredible drive in golf isn't just about hitting the ball far—it's about having a clear target and executing confidently. Similarly, a leader must articulate a compelling vision, aligning the team toward a common goal.

A golfer hesitantly steps onto the tee will likely hit a weak drive. A leader without conviction will struggle to inspire others. Authentic leadership begins with an unwavering belief in the mission—and the ability to communicate that belief in a way that rallies an entire organization.

Cultivating and Sustaining Motivation

Motivation is like a golfer's rhythm—it must be cultivated, maintained, and sometimes reignited. Leaders who understand how to sustain motivation—both in themselves and their teams—create organizations that thrive under pressure and continuously improve.

Set Clear and Meaningful Goals: Just as a golfer lines up

their shot with a specific target in mind, leaders must ensure their teams have clear, inspiring, and achievable objectives.

Break Down Goals into Manageable Steps: The best golfers focus on one shot at a time rather than getting overwhelmed by the entire round. Leaders must do the same—breaking down ambitious visions into actionable, attainable steps.

Maintain a Positive Mindset: Golf is as mental as physical, and the same applies to leadership. A leader cultivating optimism, resilience, and a can-do attitude fosters an environment where success becomes the expectation, not just the goal.

The Role of Ambition in Achieving Success

Ambition fuels both championship golfers and exceptional leaders. Without it, there's no reason to improve, push forward, or aim higher.

Ambition Drives Innovation and Growth: The best golfers don't settle—they constantly refine their technique, take on new challenges, and strive for perfection.

The best leaders do the same—continually seeking innovation, pushing boundaries, and setting higher standards.

Setting High Standards and Expectations: Ambitious leaders don't just push themselves—they challenge their teams to exceed expectations. They inspire a culture of excellence where everyone is driven to perform at their best.

Overcoming Challenges with Determination: In golf and leadership, obstacles are inevitable. Ambition drives leaders to overcome challenges, adapt to setbacks, and emerge stronger.

Inspiring Teams to Share in the Vision

The strongest drives in golf aren't just about power, direction, and precision. Likewise, in leadership, a vision is only as strong as the leader's ability to communicate and align the team around it.

Communicate a Compelling Vision: Why does this goal matter? Great leaders don't just set objectives; they connect them to a larger purpose, making every team member feel part of something greater.

Engage and Empower Team Members: A golfer can't rely solely on their drive; they must follow through with strong execution. Leaders can't just give orders; they must empower their team with trust, collaboration, and responsibility.

Lead by Example: The most outstanding leaders don't demand excellence—they embody it. Their ambition, work ethic, and drive become the model that inspires those around them.

Driving Toward Success

A golfer's drive isn't just about the swing—it's about setting the course for what comes next. The same is true for leaders.

The most successful leaders don't just work hard—they inspire, guide, and cultivate a sense of shared ambition. A leader's motivation and ambition create the foundation for long-term success, like a well-executed drive that sets up the perfect approach.

So, as you step up to the tee—or into your leadership role—swing with confidence, aim with purpose, and drive forward with relentless ambition.

Your team—and your success—depends on it.

5

Mastering the Short Game – Attention to Detail in Leadership

Winning the Round One Stroke at a Time

Picture this: You're standing over a tricky five-foot putt. The crowd is silent, the pressure is mounting, and the entire round may come down to this single stroke. It's not about power anymore. It's about precision, control, and focus. A slight miscalculation in speed or angle and your ball lips out. A perfectly executed stroke, and you walk away with confidence, one step closer to victory.

In golf, the short game—the art of putting, chipping, and close-range shots—is where championships are won or lost. You can crush the most extended drives, but those big swings mean nothing if you can't execute the short shots with precision.

Leadership operates the same way. The details matter. A leader may have a bold vision and an ambitious strategy, but the big picture falls apart if they fail to carefully execute the small, daily decisions. Just as the best golfers refine their short game to eliminate costly errors, great leaders pay attention to the finer points of their leadership—how they communicate, how they handle feedback, and how they make small but impactful choices that shape the culture and direction of their team.

Success in golf and leadership is rarely about one big moment—consistent execution in the details.

The Short Game in Golf: Where Precision Reigns

Power may get you to the green, but precision determines whether you walk away with a birdie or a bogey.

The Importance of Accuracy: When you're putting or chipping, every detail counts—the break of the green, the slope, the distance, the speed. Even a fraction of an inch can distinguish between a perfect shot and a costly mistake. The same is true in leadership—when made with care, small decisions lead to big successes.

High Stakes in Small Actions: A drive that veers slightly off course can often be recovered, but a missed three-foot putt?

That one stings. In leadership, a poor decision on a significant project might be forgivable. However, neglecting small daily responsibilities, failing to communicate appropriately, or overlooking small details can erode trust and credibility over time.

In the short game, great golfers separate themselves from the rest of the pack. And in leadership, attention to detail distinguishes great leaders from average ones.

Attention to Detail in Leadership: Small Moves, Big Impact

Leadership is filled with small but critical moments—a carefully worded email, a timely recognition of an employee's hard work, or a well-prepared response to a challenge. These moments shape culture, build trust, and inspire excellence.

The Significance of Small Decisions: Leaders who understand the power of small details recognize that a careless interaction, a poorly thought-out response, or a missed opportunity to address an issue can have long-term consequences.

Building Trust and Credibility: Just as golfers build confidence by perfecting their short game, leaders build trust by consistently demonstrating precision in their words and actions. When leaders show they care about the small things, it sends a message: Excellence matters here.

Attention to detail is not about micromanaging—it's about being intentional. It's about ensuring that every small action aligns with the organization's long-term goals.

The Link Between Golf's Short Game and Leadership's Fine-Tuned Execution

In golf and leadership, success isn't accidental—it results from careful, strategic decision-making.

Strategic Consideration: A golfer carefully assesses every putt, chip, and delicate touch around the green to make the shot and set up the next move. Similarly, a leader must ensure that every small action contributes to the broader mission.

Continuous Improvement: No golfer is naturally gifted at the short game. It takes hours of practice, adjustment, and refinement. The same applies to leadership.

Great leaders constantly refine their decision-making, improve their communication skills, and sharpen their awareness of the small but significant details that shape their organization.

Golfers who overlook their short game struggle to score well, and leaders who overlook attention to detail struggle to build sustainable success.

The Ripple Effect of Small Actions

A single well-placed putt can turn a good round into a great one. In the same way, a single well-thought-out decision—no matter how minor—can set off a chain reaction of favorable results in an organization.

The Compounding Effect: A golfer who masterfully controls their putts and chips gains an edge over time. Likewise, a leader who consistently makes thoughtful, detail-oriented decisions builds credibility and trust, strengthening the organization.

Preventing Major Issues: A tiny adjustment in putting grip or stance can avoid a string of missed putts in golf. In leadership, catching small inefficiencies, addressing minor communication gaps, and refining processes early can prevent more significant problems from spiraling out of control.

Details are not distractions—they are the foundation of excellence.

Leadership Lessons from Golf's Short Game

Mastering the short game in golf requires discipline, patience, and precision—all qualities that exceptional leaders cultivate in their approach.

Focus and Discipline: A short putt requires total concentration. There is no room for distraction, second-guessing, or hesitation. The same is true in leadership—great leaders remain focused and disciplined in their attention to detail.

Strategic Patience: Not every putt should be aggressively attacked. Some require a gentle, measured approach. Leaders must know when to push forward, step back, and reassess. Rushed decisions often lead to mistakes, but calculated patience leads to success.

Learning from Every Experience: Golfers track their mistakes, analyze their strokes, and refine their techniques. The best leaders do the same—they reflect on decisions, learn from past successes and failures, and continuously improve their ability to manage details precisely.

It's not about obsessing over every small thing—it's about understanding which details matter most and executing them excellently.

The Game Is Won in the Details

Golf's short game is where champions are made. A golfer who excels in putting and chipping doesn't just avoid mistakes—they capitalize on opportunities, eliminate unnecessary errors, and consistently put themselves in winning positions.

The same is true in leadership.

The best leaders don't just think about the big ideas, the grand vision, or the long-term strategy. They recognize that their success is built on how well they execute the small but critical moments—each conversation, decision, and interaction.

Leadership isn't just about where you want to go—it's about how you handle the details along the way.

So the next time you face a seemingly small decision in leadership—an employee concern, a brief interaction, a minor strategic adjustment—approach it with the same precision a golfer brings to the short game.

Because, in the end, success isn't about the big swings. It's about the small, precise moves that make the most significant difference.

6

The Importance of Practice – Continuous Improvement in Leadership

The Relentless Pursuit of Mastery

Imagine standing on the driving range, a bucket of golf balls at your feet. You take your stance, adjust your grip, and swing repeatedly. The first few shots might not be perfect, but with every repetition, you refine your technique, correct your form, and build consistency. It's a process, and perfection doesn't come overnight.

This is the essence of golf practice. Mastery is built through repetition, reflection, and relentless refinement. It's not just about swinging harder—it's about swinging smarter, learning from each shot, and making adjustments to improve over time.

Leadership follows the same principle. The best leaders don't rely on natural talent alone—they commit themselves to constant learning, growth, and self-improvement. Just as a golfer fine-tunes their swing, leaders must refine their ability to communicate, make decisions, and adapt to an ever-changing environment. Like success in golf, leadership success is not about hitting one great shot—it's about consistently improving over time.

The Role of Practice in Golf: Repetition, Adaptation, and Mastery

No golfer becomes great by accident. Behind every championship win are countless hours of practice—hitting thousands of balls, fine-tuning mechanics, and adjusting to different course conditions.

Perfecting Technique: Golfers don't just swing aimlessly; they break down their mechanics—grip, stance, posture, backswing, follow-through—and refine each element until excellence becomes second nature.

Adapting to Different Conditions: No two courses or rounds are identical. Wind, temperature, terrain, and pressure impact a golfer's game. The best players practice in varied conditions, preparing for every possible challenge.

Great golfers understand that practice isn't about repeating mistakes but identifying weaknesses, making corrections, and ensuring steady progress. This same mindset is crucial for leaders.

Continuous Improvement in Leadership: The Discipline of Lifelong Learning Just as golfers must fine-tune their mechanics, leaders must continuously develop their skills to stay sharp and effective.

Learning and Adapting: The world of leadership is ever-changing. New challenges, evolving industries, and shifting team dynamics require leaders to stay flexible and open to growth. A leader who stops learning is a leader who starts falling behind.

Skill Development: Golfers work on driving, chipping, putting, and course management. Leaders must develop communication, decision-making, emotional intelligence, and strategic thinking. Both require dedication to constant refinement.

Leadership, like golf, is not about reaching a finish line—it's about continuous improvement and lifelong mastery.

The Link Between Golf Practice and Leadership Growth

Great golfers don't just show up and play—they develop habits that fuel improvement. The same is true for leaders.

Discipline and Consistency: Improvement doesn't come from occasional bursts of effort. It's the daily, consistent habits that create long-term success. Just as a golfer builds muscle memory through repetition, leaders develop their leadership instincts through consistent skill application, reflection, and adjustment.

Embracing Feedback: Golfers rely on coaches, video analysis, and self-reflection to correct their flaws. Leaders, too, must welcome feedback—from mentors, peers, and team members—to refine their approach.

Setting Goals and Measuring Progress: Every golf practice session has a purpose—lowering putts per round, increasing driving accuracy, and reducing errors. Leaders must do the same—set development goals, track growth, and measure their impact on their teams and organizations.

Improvement in golf or leadership is not random—it's intentional, structured, and focused on progress.

The Impact of Continuous Learning on Leadership Success

The most significant players in golf never stop refining their skills, no matter how many championships they've won. The same is true for great leaders.

Staying Competitive: Golfers who fail to adapt to changing course conditions struggle to keep up, and leaders who fail to evolve with the demands of their industry risk falling behind their competitors. The best leaders, like the best golfers, remain students of the game.

Inspiring Others: When leaders demonstrate a commitment to growth, they inspire their teams to do the same. A culture of continuous improvement starts at the top—when leaders prioritize learning, they encourage their organizations to embrace development, innovation, and excellence.

Building a Culture of Continuous Improvement

A golfer's improvement is personal, but leadership improvement should be contagious. Great leaders don't just grow themselves—they create an environment where their entire team is driven to improve.

Encouraging Open Communication: Feedback from a

coach is invaluable in golf. In leadership, teams must feel comfortable sharing insights, ideas, and constructive criticism. A leader who listens fosters a culture where continuous learning is the norm.

Providing Learning Opportunities: Leaders should invest in professional development, just as golfers invest in coaching, equipment, and training. Workshops, mentorship programs, and learning resources empower teams to grow.

Recognizing and Rewarding Growth: A golfer who improves their short game sees better scores. In leadership, growth must be acknowledged and rewarded—celebrating small wins reinforces a constant learning and improvement culture.

Lessons from Leaders Who Never Stopped Learning

The world's most successful leaders share a common trait: relentless curiosity and a hunger for growth.

Warren Buffett: Despite being one of the wealthiest individuals in the world, Buffett spends most of his time reading, studying, and expanding his knowledge. His success is rooted in his commitment to lifelong learning.

Indra Nooyi: As the former CEO of PepsiCo, Nooyi

constantly sought new knowledge—whether through education, experience, or mentorship—which allowed her to navigate complex business transformations with confidence.

Bill Gates: Even after stepping away from Microsoft, Gates remains a voracious reader and student of the world, using his continuous learning to drive impactful global initiatives.

These leaders didn't stop growing once they achieved success—they recognized that authentic leadership is a lifelong learning, refining, and evolving process.

Greatness is Built on Practice

In golf, there are no shortcuts to mastery. The best players commit to practice, embrace feedback, and refine their skills daily.

In leadership, the same rules apply.

A leader's success is not determined by a single breakthrough moment—it's shaped by the small, consistent efforts they make every day to improve, learn, and grow.

Like the best golfers, leaders never settle for "good enough." They strive for excellence, seek feedback, and push themselves to be better than they were yesterday.

So whether you're standing on the driving range or leading a team, remember: The game isn't won in a single moment—it's won through dedication, continuous improvement, and the commitment to practice every day.

7

Handling Hazards – Overcoming Obstacles in Leadership

Navigating the Rough: Turning Challenges into Opportunities

Imagine stepping up to the tee on a pristine fairway, feeling confident as you send the ball soaring down the course—only to watch it land in a deep bunker or, worse, splash into a water hazard. Suddenly, the game has changed. You're no longer playing from a position of strength; now, you must adapt, recalibrate, and strategize to recover.

Golf, like leadership, is not played on a perfectly smooth surface. Hazards are inevitable—sand traps, water hazards, deep rough, and unpredictable weather challenge a golfer's ability to stay composed and make wise decisions. The best players don't panic or dwell on mistakes; they assess their situation, adjust their approach, and confidently execute their next move.

Leaders face similar challenges. Economic downturns, internal conflicts, shifting markets, and unforeseen crises are the hazards of leadership. Like in golf, how leaders respond to obstacles defines their ability to lead successfully. Those who can maintain composure, think strategically, and adapt to changing conditions will not only navigate challenges but also emerge stronger.

Hazards in Golf: When the Game Doesn't Go as Planned

A well-executed drive may set up a straightforward approach to the green, but golf is unpredictable. Even the best shots can land under challenging spots, and the actual test of skill is not just hitting great shots but recovering from difficult ones.

Recognizing and Assessing Hazards: Before taking the next shot, a golfer must evaluate the risk, consider the best escape route, and decide whether to take an aggressive or conservative approach. Leaders, too, must recognize when challenges arise, assess their impact, and determine the most strategic path forward.

Strategic Adaptation: A golfer in a bunker may need to change their club, alter their stance, or adjust their swing to escape. Similarly, a leader facing a crisis must adapt their strategy, shift priorities, and remain flexible. The key is not to let frustration or fear dictate decisions but to stay focused on the long game.

In golf and leadership, challenges are not a matter of "if" but "when." How one responds is what separates the great from the average.

Overcoming Obstacles in Leadership: The Power of Resilience and Adaptability

Just as golfers face water hazards and sand traps, leaders face obstacles that test their patience, skills, and decision-making abilities. The best leaders understand that setbacks are not roadblocks—they are opportunities for learning and growth.

Identifying and Understanding Challenges: Whether dealing with financial setbacks, operational failures, or unexpected personnel issues, leaders must approach problems with clarity, logic, and a willingness to adapt. Ignoring challenges doesn't make them disappear—addressing them head-on is the only way to move forward.

Resilience in the Face of Setbacks: A lousy shot into the rough can throw off an entire round, but great golfers don't let it shake their confidence. Similarly, resilient leaders don't allow one failure or challenge to define their leadership. They regroup, reassess, and focus on what comes next.

Leaders who develop resilience stay calm under pressure, inspire team confidence, and focus on long-term goals, even when short-term setbacks arise.

The Link Between Golf Hazards and Leadership Challenges

Both golfers and leaders must approach challenges not as disasters but as puzzles to be solved strategically.

Strategic Problem-Solving: A golfer in a challenging position must weigh their options—play it safe or take a calculated risk. Leaders, too, must analyze the risks, resources, and potential outcomes before deciding on a course of action.

Learning from Experience: Every time a golfer recovers from a difficult situation, they build confidence and knowledge for the next time it happens. Leaders who have faced adversity develop a deeper understanding of their strengths, weaknesses, and ability to navigate complex situations.

Both golf and leadership teach the importance of thinking ahead, staying flexible, and focusing on progress rather than perfection.

The Importance of Resilience and Adaptability in Achieving Success

A golfer who lets one nasty hole define their game will struggle to stay competitive. The same is true for leadership—setbacks are inevitable, but success comes from how leaders recover and adapt.

Building Confidence and Trust: Leaders who remain composed under pressure instill confidence in their teams. Employees look to leaders for guidance during difficult times, and those who stay steady, solution-focused, and resilient build trust that strengthens the entire organization.

Fostering a Culture of Resilience: The best golfers don't dwell on mistakes; they learn from them. The best leaders foster a culture where challenges are viewed as learning experiences, not failures. By encouraging collaboration, supporting innovation, and leading with a growth mindset, they create an organization capable of overcoming any obstacle.

Outstanding leadership isn't about avoiding hazards but navigating them skillfully and helping others do the same.

Strategies for Overcoming Challenges and Setbacks

Leaders must employ proactive strategies and a resilient mindset to navigate challenges successfully.

Proactive Problem-Solving: Anticipate potential hazards before they happen. Just as a golfer studies a course before playing, leaders must analyze possible risks and develop contingency plans.

Focusing on Long-Term Goals: Don't let short-term setbacks derail the bigger vision. The best leaders focus on the mission and adjust tactics to stay on course.

Leveraging Team Strengths: Overcoming challenges isn't a solo effort. Strong leaders recognize their team members' skills and bring them together for creative solutions.

When leaders think strategically, maintain perspective, and use setbacks as learning opportunities, challenges become stepping stones rather than roadblocks.

Examples of Leaders Who Turned Obstacles into Opportunities

Some of the world's most successful leaders faced significant setbacks—but rather than letting those obstacles define them, they turned them into opportunities for growth and transformation.

Nelson Mandela: Imprisoned for 27 years, Mandela used his time to learn, strategize, and build resilience, ultimately leading South Africa through a peaceful transition from apartheid to democracy.

Howard Schultz (Starbucks): When Starbucks's sales declined during the 2008 financial crisis, Schultz returned as CEO, implemented strategic changes, and revitalized the brand.

Oprah Winfrey: Overcoming a difficult childhood and early career setbacks, Oprah used her challenges as motivation to create an empire focused on empowerment, education, and social change.

These leaders understood that adversity is not an endpoint but an opportunity to innovate, grow, and emerge stronger.

Hazards Don't Define You—How You Handle Them Does

Every golfer will encounter a hazard at some point, just as every leader will face setbacks. What matters isn't avoiding challenges but developing the resilience, adaptability, and strategic mindset to overcome them.

The most successful leaders—like the best golfers—don't let a lousy shot ruin their game. They analyze, adjust, and move forward with confidence.

So the next time you face a hazard—whether on the course or in leadership—take a deep breath, assess your options, and make your next move purposefully.

After all, the best leaders, like the best golfers, know that the only absolute failure is the failure to keep going.

8

Playing with Patience – The Role of Patience in Leadership

The Steady Hand: Why Patience Wins the Game

A golfer stands over a long, breaking putt, reading the slope, feeling the wind, and resisting the temptation to rush the shot. The crowd is silent. The tournament is on the line. Instead of hurrying through the moment, the golfer breathes, focuses, and trusts the process—knowing that the best results come from careful preparation, calm execution, and a steady hand.

This is the essence of patience in golf. Success doesn't come from rushed swings or impulsive decisions; it comes from composure, consistency, and staying focused on the long game.

Leadership operates the same way. The most effective leaders don't react hastily to challenges, force results, or demand immediate success. Instead, they develop their teams, cultivate their vision, and allow time for progress to unfold naturally. Like a seasoned golfer who understands that a round is won one stroke at a time, great leaders recognize that true success is a journey, not a single moment of achievement.

The Role of Patience in Golf: Mastering the Mental Game

Golf is as much a mental challenge as it is a physical one. A golfer's ability to remain patient can mean the difference between recovering from a nasty hole or unraveling under frustration.

Staying Calm Under Pressure: Every round of golf has highs and lows—a missed putt, a bad lie, an unlucky bounce. Patient golfers understand that overreacting to setbacks only makes things worse. They stay composed, analyze the situation, and focus on what comes next rather than dwelling on mistakes.

Taking the Long View: A single lousy hole does not define a golfer's final score, just as a single setback does not determine a leader's ultimate success. Golfers who approach each shot patiently and precisely give themselves the best chance of succeeding over the entire round.

The best golfers recognize that momentary frustration must never override long-term strategy. The same is true for leaders.

Patience in Leadership: Cultivating Growth, Strategy, and Vision

Like a great golfer, a strong leader understands that success takes time. Rushing a process, forcing a solution, or demanding instant results often leads to frustration and failure.

Developing Teams Over Time: Leaders must be patient in nurturing their teams' skills, confidence, and trust. Growth doesn't happen overnight, and a leader's role is to provide guidance, support, and opportunities for learning—understanding that long-term development is more valuable than short-term fixes.

Trusting the Process: Whether launching a new initiative, implementing change, or tackling an ambitious project, leaders must resist the urge to seek immediate results. The actual impact often takes months or even years to materialize. The best leaders stay the course, make adjustments when necessary, and remain committed to the bigger picture.

Allowing Vision to Unfold: Every outstanding achievement—building a company, leading a movement, or creating lasting change—requires patience. Leaders who rush to see results often make compromises that weaken their vision, while those who patiently nurture their ideas ensure that their work stands the test of time.

Just as a golfer carefully reads the green before making a putt, a great leader takes the time to understand, plan, and execute with intention.

The Link Between Patience in Golf and Leadership

Golf and leadership require a steady mindset and a willingness to play the long game.

Dealing with Setbacks: Every golfer will face difficult shots—a drive into the trees, a missed par-saving putt, a round that doesn't go as planned. The ability to recover and refocus separates great players from those who let frustration take over. The same applies to leadership—setbacks, failures, and delays are inevitable, but a leader's patience and resilience determine their ability to keep moving forward.

Strategic Decision-Making: A rushed shot in golf can turn a bad situation into disastrous. Likewise, leaders who make impulsive decisions risk long-term damage to their teams and organizations. Patient leaders take the time to gather input, weigh their options, and consider the best course of action before making essential choices.

Building Enduring Success: Golf is not about winning a single hole—it's about playing well over an entire round. Leadership follows the same principle: lasting success is built on well-thought-out decisions, careful planning, and steady progress over time.

Leaders, like golfers, must resist the temptation to rush success and instead focus on consistency, perseverance, and trust in their process.

How Patience Leads to Long-Term Success

Patience isn't just about waiting—it's about understanding that success is built step by step.

Foundation for Sustainable Growth: Leaders who prioritize long-term impact over immediate gratification create more stable, innovative organizations and are better positioned for the future.

Resilience and Endurance: Patience allows leaders to confidently navigate setbacks rather than reacting emotionally or making impulsive changes. They recognize that delays and challenges are part of the journey, not reasons to abandon their strategy.

Patience is not passive but an active commitment to growth, strategy, and thoughtful decision-making.

How Leaders Can Cultivate Patience

Encourage a Long-Term Perspective: Help your team see beyond short-term challenges by reminding them of the bigger picture. Patience is more manageable when everyone understands the journey.

Set Realistic Expectations: Expecting instant results often leads to frustration. By communicating realistic timelines and potential roadblocks, leaders help their teams develop a patient, steady mindset.

Celebrate Small Wins: While patience focuses on long-term success, recognizing progress keeps motivation high—every step forward—no matter how small—is part of the journey.

Great leaders don't demand instant success—they build a foundation for success to unfold over time.

Lessons from Golf on the Power of Patience

Golf teaches patience better than almost any other sport.

Staying Calm Under Pressure: Whether it's a critical putt on the 18th hole or a high-stakes leadership decision, staying composed leads to better outcomes.

Embracing the Process: The best golfers focus on one shot at a time rather than getting overwhelmed by the final score. The best leaders focus on incremental progress, knowing that great things take Patience is not just a trait but a skill that can be developed and strengthened.

Practice Mindful Decision-Making: Take a step back before reacting to a situation. Analyze the facts, consider the long-term impact, and make choices aligning with your vision time.

Learning from Mistakes: A golfer who lets one lousy shot ruin their focus will struggle to recover. A leader who sees mistakes as learning opportunities will improve and grow stronger.

Patience is not just about waiting—it's about learning, adapting, and playing the long game with confidence and intention.

The Power of Patience in Leadership

In golf, the most patient players control their emotions, make wise decisions, and focus on the long-term result rather than a single moment.

In leadership, patience is the difference between short-term gains and long-term success.

Leaders who develop patience build resilient teams, make thoughtful decisions, and create a vision that endures.

So the next time you feel impatient with a slow-moving project, a challenging situation, or the pace of progress, remember:

Like every great golfer, every great leader understands that patience isn't just a virtue—it's the key to winning the long game.

9

The Ethics of the Game – Leading with Fairness and Respect

Integrity on the Course, Integrity in Leadership

A golfer lines up their shot, the ball resting on the fringe of the green. No referees are watching, no officials keeping track—only the player's conscience dictates their next move. Golf is one of the few sports where honesty and self-regulation are not just expected but required. Players are responsible for calling penalties on themselves, respecting the course, and treating competitors fairly.

This level of integrity is what sets golf apart. It's a game that demands not just skill but character.

Leadership is no different. The most effective leaders hold themselves to the highest ethical standards, not because they are being watched, but because it's the right thing to do. Fairness, respect, and integrity aren't just desirable traits in leadership—they are the foundation of trust, collaboration, and long-term success.

Leaders, like golfers, are judged by their results and how they achieve them.

The Ethics of Golf: A Game Built on Trust

While most sports rely on referees to enforce rules, golf places ethical responsibility directly on the player. The best golfers don't just aim for low scores—they uphold the spirit of the game through honesty, respect, and fair play.

Fair Play: The Ultimate Test of Integrity

In golf, fair play is not just about following the rules—it's about adhering to a personal standard of integrity. Golfers are expected to play their ball as it lies, even if no one is watching. This principle underscores a valuable leadership lesson: doing the right thing, even without external pressure.

Respect for Competitors and the Game

Golf culture is built on mutual respect—players remain silent when others take a shot, repair divots, and leave the course better than they found it. Leaders can learn from this by creating a workplace where respect is not just encouraged but ingrained—where people listen, support one another, and contribute to a healthy, thriving environment.

Integrity and Accountability

The heart of golf's ethics is integrity—players are expected to report their own penalties, even when they work against them. In leadership, this translates to owning mistakes, making decisions based on values rather than convenience, and being transparent with employees and stakeholders. Leaders who act with integrity earn the trust and respect of those they lead.

Great golfers don't just win—they win the right way. The same goes for great leaders.

Leading with Fairness: The Cornerstone of Ethical Leadership

Just as golf demands fair play, leadership requires fairness in decision-making, opportunity distribution, and conflict resolution. A leader who plays favorites, shifts blame, or makes inconsistent decisions erodes trust and weakens the organization.

Creating an Even-Playing Field

Just as golfers play by the same rules regardless of rank or reputation, ethical leaders ensure that opportunities, promotions, and rewards are based on merit, not bias. They foster an environment where everyone has a fair chance to succeed.

Making Decisions with Integrity

Ethical leaders don't take shortcuts for personal gain or prioritize short-term wins over long-term sustainability. Leaders must be willing to make difficult but ethical choices, like a golfer who plays the ball honestly, even in a challenging position.

Handling Conflict with Objectivity

When disputes arise on the golf course, players rely on the game's rules rather than emotions. Ethical leaders apply the same principle—resolving conflicts based on fairness, transparency, and respect rather than favoritism or personal interests.

A leader's fairness builds trust within a team and strengthens an organization's culture.

Respect: A Leadership Quality That Inspires Loyalty

Golfers respect not only the game but also their competitors, the course, and the traditions that make the sport what it is. Similarly, leaders who cultivate a culture of respect create organizations where employees feel valued, heard, and motivated to contribute their best work.

Listening to Team Members

Respect in leadership starts with listening. Leaders who actively engage with their teams, seek input and acknowledge diverse perspectives foster a workplace where everyone feels valued.

Treating Others with Dignity

Just as golfers never interfere with an opponent's shot, ethical leaders ensure that every team member is treated with dignity, regardless of rank or role. They create an inclusive environment where collaboration, rather than competition, drives success.

Recognizing Contributions

Golfers acknowledge their competitors' great shots with a nod or a handshake. Leaders should do the same by recognizing their teams' efforts, celebrating achievements, and ensuring that credit is given where it is due.

A culture of respect isn't just about being polite—it's about empowering people to do their best work.

The Long-Term Impact of Ethical Leadership

Ethical leadership doesn't just feel good—it leads to tangible success. Organizations led with integrity:

Attract top talent who want to work in an environment based on trust and fairness. Foster innovation and collaboration because employees feel safe sharing ideas.

Achieve long-term stability because leaders make decisions that prioritize sustainability over short-term gains.

Companies with strong ethical leadership don't just perform well in the short run—they build lasting legacies.

Lessons from Ethical Leaders Who Led with Integrity

The best leaders, like the best golfers, are remembered for what they achieved and how they achieved it.

Nelson Mandela:

Despite decades of imprisonment and oppression, Mandela led South Africa with forgiveness, fairness, and an unwavering commitment to justice. He believed in leading by example, respecting others, and building a future based on integrity rather than revenge.

Mary Barra (General Motors):

As CEO of GM, Barra transformed the company's culture by prioritizing ethics, transparency, and accountability—especially during the ignition switch crisis. She took responsibility, implemented safety reforms, and rebuilt trust in the company's leadership.

Paul Polman (Unilever):

Polman redefined corporate leadership by prioritizing sustainability and ethical business practices over short-term profits. He believed companies should serve society, not just shareholders, and embedded these values into Unilever's long-term strategy.

These leaders proved that doing the right thing is not just good ethics—it's good business.

Leadership Is Defined by Ethics, Not Just Results

Golfers are remembered not just for their victories but also for how they conduct themselves on the course. The same holds for leadership.

Like a great golfer, a great leader follows the rules, respects others, and plays with integrity—whether anyone is watching or not.

So the next time you're faced with a tough decision, ask yourself: Am I being fair in my judgment?

Am I treating others with respect?

Am I leading with integrity—even if no one is watching?

Because in the end, leaders, like golfers, are not just measured by their achievements—but by the character they demonstrate along the way.

10

Finishing Strong – Leaving a Lasting Leadership Legacy

The Final Stretch – Why the Finish Matters

The sun begins to set over the final hole of a championship tournament. The leader-board is tight, and every shot in these last few moments will define the outcome. A golfer who has played well all day knows that none of it will matter if they can't finish strong. The closing holes separate the great from the good.

Leadership works the same way. A leader's legacy isn't just built on their first big success or the strides made early in their career—it's defined by how they conclude their tenure and the impact they leave behind.

Like the greatest golfers, the most outstanding leaders don't just seek short-term victories. They think about what they will leave behind, ensuring that the organization, the people, and the vision they've nurtured thrive long after they are gone.

The Power of Finishing Strong in Golf Turning a Good Round into a Great One

A golfer can play well throughout the day, but the final few holes often make or break the scorecard. Those who stay focused, adapt to the pressure, and execute precisely are remembered.

Delivering Under Pressure

The best golfers thrive in high-stakes moments. They don't let fatigue, nerves, or setbacks dictate their final shots. Instead, they rely on discipline, skill, and strategy to finish the round as strong as they started.

Creating a Lasting Impression

The final strokes on the last few holes leave an impression on fans, fellow competitors, and history. A clutch performance under pressure cements a golfer's reputation. How a golfer finishes often defines their career, highlights, and legacy.

In leadership, the same principles apply. **Building a Legacy That Lasts in Leadership Ensuring Long-Term Success**

Just as a golfer must plan for a strong finish, leaders must prepare their organizations to succeed long after they leave. This means developing future leaders, establishing sustainable processes, and embedding core values into the culture.

Impacting People, Not Just Profits

A leader's most significant legacy isn't found in profit margins or financial reports—it's in the people they mentored, the culture they built, and the lives they changed. Ethical, people-centered leadership creates an enduring impact beyond a leader's tenure.

Fostering Innovation and Continuous Growth

Leaders who leave a legacy of innovation ensure their organization remains dynamic, adaptable, and forward-thinking. By fostering a continuous learning and improvement culture, they empower teams to keep evolving long after they step down.

A strong leadership legacy isn't just about maintaining what's been built—it's about ensuring future success.

The Leadership Lessons from Golf's Greatest Finishes Consistency Defines Greatness

A strong finish isn't an accident—it's the result of consistency, discipline, and preparation. Just as a golfer stays focused throughout the round, leaders must remain true to their values, commitments, and vision until the end.

Reflection and Adaptation Are Keys

The best golfers analyze their previous shots, learn from mistakes, and adjust their approach to finish strong. Leaders who reflect on their journey, learn from their experiences and make necessary adjustments in their final stages leave behind a more resilient and prepared organization.

Excellence in the Final Moments Shapes the Story

Just as a golfer is remembered for a winning putt on the 18th hole, a leader is remembered for closing out their tenure. Those who lead with excellence in their final days leave a lasting impression on their teams and inspire future leaders to carry the torch.

Examples of Leaders Who Finished Strong

Steve Jobs (Apple Inc.) – *A Vision That Outlived Him*

Steve Jobs left Apple twice—once in exile and once in legacy. After returning to the company in the late 1990s, Jobs transformed Apple into one of the most successful brands in history. His final years were spent ensuring that Apple could thrive without him. Before his passing, he established a culture of innovation, a commitment to design excellence, and a leadership structure that carried Apple to new heights, even after he was gone.

Mahatma Gandhi – *The Legacy of Peace and Resistance*

Gandhi didn't just fight for India's independence—he fought for a lasting vision of unity, peace, and self-governance. His final years ensured that India's freedom was not just political but built on principles of nonviolence and justice that would endure for generations. His leadership didn't just free a nation; it changed the world's understanding of resistance and ethics.

Jacinda Ardern (Former Prime Minister of New Zealand) – *Leading with Empathy*

Jacinda Ardern symbolized compassionate and resilient leadership during crises, including the Christchurch mosque shootings and the COVID-19 pandemic. Her decision to step down was not a retreat but a reflection of her belief that leadership is about knowing when to pass the baton. Her tenure was marked by progressive policies, inclusive leadership, and a legacy that inspires leaders to lead with strength and empathy.

These leaders understood that authentic leadership is not about retaining power but about ensuring the right foundations are set for the future.

How to Finish Strong as a Leader Mentor and Develop Future Leaders

A great leader's final responsibility is to develop those who will continue the work. Investing time in mentor-ship, coaching, and leadership development ensures that their values, vision, and principles live on.

Embed Core Values in the Organization

Just as golfers don't change their fundamentals on the final holes, leaders should reinforce core values in their last days. These values—whether integrity, innovation, or accountability—must be deeply ingrained in the organization's culture.

Foster a Culture of Continuous Growth

The best leaders create self-sustaining teams that continue evolving and innovating. By encouraging learning, adaptability, and a continuous improvement mindset, they ensure that success is not dependent on one person but embedded in the organization's DNA.

Leave the Organization Better Than You Found It

Leaders should aim to make decisions that set up long-term success, not just short-term wins. Whether through structural improvements, cultural shifts, or visionary strategy, the goal should be to leave a lasting, positive impact.

The True Measure of a Leader

Golfers are remembered not just for how they started but also for how they closed the game.

A leader's legacy is the same. It's not just about what they built but what they left behind.

So, ask yourself:

- Will your organization be more potent after you leave?
- Will your team feel inspired by the culture and vision you've nurtured?
- Will your leadership principles continue to guide decisions long after you're gone?

The most outstanding leaders are not defined by their tenure but by their impact. Like in golf, the most crucial shot is often the last one you take.

So make it count. Finish strong. Leave a legacy that lasts.

Epilogue

The Leadership Fairway: A Continuous Journey

Overview: The Continuous Journey of Leadership and Golf

Leadership and golf are profoundly similar as continuous journeys of growth, learning, and striving for excellence. Just as a golfer never truly "finishes" perfecting their game, a leader constantly evolves, learns from experiences, and refines their approach. Both disciplines require dedication, resilience, and a commitment to constant improvement. This chapter reflects on the journey of leadership, drawing parallels with the ongoing pursuit of mastery in golf, and emphasizes the importance of embracing this journey as a lifelong process.

The Continuous Nature of Golf: A Quest for Mastery Endless Improvement:

No matter how skilled a player becomes in golf, there is always room for improvement. Golfers continually work on refining their swing, improving their short game, and mastering the mental aspects of the sport. This relentless pursuit of betterment keeps golfers engaged, driving them to practice regularly and learn from every round they play.

Learning from Every Shot:

Every shot in golf offers an opportunity to learn. Whether it's a well-executed drive or a missed putt, golfers analyze their performance, seeking insights that can help them improve. This reflective process is vital to continuous growth, allowing golfers to adjust their techniques and strategies.

Leadership as a Never-Ending Journey of Growth Ongoing Learning and Development:

Leadership, like golf, is a field where growth and learning never cease. Leaders must continually develop their skills, adapt to new challenges, and expand their knowledge. This might involve learning new management techniques, understanding emerging trends, or gaining deeper insights into human behavior and motivation. The best leaders embrace this lifelong learning journey and view each experience as a stepping stone to greater wisdom.

Resilience and Adaptability:

Just as golfers must adapt to changing conditions on the course, leaders must be resilient and adaptable in the face of evolving circumstances. Whether navigating a crisis, leading through change, or managing a diverse team, leaders must constantly adjust their approach, learning from each situation to become more effective. This adaptability is crucial for sustained leadership success.

The Parallel Between Golf and Leadership: Commitment to Excellence Pursuit of Perfection:

Both golf and leadership involve a pursuit of perfection, even though true perfection may be unattainable. The perfect round is an elusive goal in golf, but the quest to achieve it drives players to push their limits. Similarly, leaders strive for excellence in their decisions, actions, and impact, knowing that this pursuit helps them and their organizations reach their fullest potential.

Reflection and Growth:

Reflection is a critical component of both golf and leadership. After each round of golf, players reflect on their performance, identifying areas for improvement.

Leaders do the same by reflecting on their leadership decisions, strategies, and outcomes. This process of reflection and self-assessment fosters continuous growth, enabling leaders to refine their approach and make better decisions in the future.

Embracing the Journey: The Path to Mastery Enjoying the Process:

One of the key lessons from both golf and leadership is the importance of enjoying the journey. While the destination—winning a tournament or achieving a leadership milestone—is essential, the real value lies in the journey. Embracing the process of learning, growing, and striving for excellence is what makes the journey fulfilling and rewarding.

Building a Legacy Through Continuous Improvement:

Leaders who commit to continuous improvement enhance their capabilities and build a lasting legacy. By modeling a commitment to growth, they inspire their teams to adopt the same mindset, creating a culture of continuous learning and excellence long after the leader's tenure. This legacy of growth and development is one of the most potent impacts a leader can leave behind.

Conclusion

The journey of leadership is much like the continuous pursuit of mastery in golf—both are lifelong processes characterized by growth, learning, and a relentless pursuit of excellence. Leaders, like golfers, must embrace the challenges, reflect on their experiences, and remain committed to improving their skills and strategies over time. Leaders can foster resilience, adaptability, and a passion for continuous improvement by viewing leadership as a never-ending journey. This mindset enhances their effectiveness and inspires those they lead, creating a ripple effect of growth and excellence that defines their legacy. Just as in golf, where the journey of improvement is ongoing, leadership is about continuously striving to improve, making a positive impact, and enjoying the process.

Key Points: The Ongoing Journey of Leadership, Staying Motivated and Inspired, and Applying Golf Principles to Leadership

The Ongoing Journey of Leadership and Personal Development Lifelong Learning and Growth:

Leadership is a continuous journey of learning and growth.

Just as golfers never stop refining their skills, influential leaders continually seek opportunities to expand their knowledge, enhance their abilities, and grow personally and professionally. This commitment to lifelong learning helps leaders stay relevant, innovative, and prepared to tackle new challenges as they arise.

Embracing Change and Evolution:

The journey of leadership requires embracing change and recognizing that growth often comes from stepping out of one's comfort zone. Leaders who view their role as an evolving process are better equipped to adapt to new circumstances, drive transformation, and confidently lead their teams through periods of uncertainty.

How to Remain Motivated and Inspired in Both Leadership and Life Setting Meaningful Goals:

Staying motivated in leadership involves setting clear, meaningful goals that align with your values and vision. These goals act as a compass, guiding your actions and providing a sense of purpose. Regularly revisiting and refining your goals helps you maintain focus and direction, which helps sustain your motivation over time.

Finding Inspiration in Challenges:

Challenges are inevitable in leadership and life, but they can also be powerful sources of inspiration. Leaders who view challenges as opportunities for growth and learning are more likely to stay motivated, even in difficult times. Leaders can maintain their enthusiasm and drive by embracing challenges and using them as fuel for personal and professional development.

Cultivating a Supportive Network:

Surrounding yourself with a supportive network of peers, mentors, and colleagues is crucial for staying motivated and inspired. These relationships provide encouragement, feedback, and different perspectives to help you navigate your leadership journey. Engaging with others who share your passion for growth and excellence fosters a sense of community and shared purpose, which can be incredibly motivating.

Encouraging Readers to Apply the Principles of Golf to Their Own Leadership Journeys

Focus on Continuous Improvement:

Just as golfers always look for ways to improve their game, leaders should focus on continuous improvement in their leadership journey. This means regularly assessing your strengths and areas for growth, seeking feedback, and making incremental changes to enhance your effectiveness. Adopting a continuous improvement mindset ensures that you're always moving forward and becoming a better leader.

Practice Patience and Persistence:

Golf teaches the importance of patience and persistence—equally vital qualities in leadership. Leaders should recognize that meaningful progress takes time and that setbacks are a natural part of the journey. By practicing patience and staying persistent in the face of challenges, you build resilience and increase your chances of long-term success.

Embrace Reflection and Learning:

Just as golfers reflect on each round to learn and improve, leaders should regularly reflect on their experiences to gain insights and grow. This reflection helps you identify what's working well, where improvements can be made, and how to adjust your strategies moving forward. By making reflection a regular part of your leadership practice, you enhance your ability to learn from successes and failures, leading to continuous development.

Conclusion

The journey of leadership is an ongoing process of personal and professional development, much like the continuous pursuit of excellence in golf. To remain motivated and inspired in leadership and life, it's important to set meaningful goals, find inspiration in challenges, and cultivate a supportive network. You can navigate leadership challenges with resilience and grace by applying the principles of golf—such as continuous improvement, patience, persistence, and reflection—to your leadership journey. This approach helps you become a more effective leader and ensures that you enjoy the journey, finding fulfillment and growth along the way. Like in golf, where each round offers new opportunities for learning and development, leadership is about embracing the journey, striving for excellence, and inspiring others to do the same.

Afterward

As I reflect on the journey that led to the creation of *The Leadership Fairway*, I am reminded of the countless rounds of golf I've witnessed and the many leaders I've had the privilege of seeing at play. Though my attempts at mastering the game of golf were met with the humbling realization that it wasn't my calling, the experiences I gained behind the camera and alongside remarkable individuals like Tommy Jacobs opened my eyes to the profound lessons the game offers.

Golf, in many ways, is a metaphor for life and leadership. It's a game of integrity, where honesty and self-discipline are paramount. It's a game of focus, where each shot requires attention and precision. It's a game of strategy, where long-term planning is as crucial as moment-to-moment decisions. And, perhaps most importantly, it's a game that teaches resilience, patience, and the importance of finishing strong.

Through the chapters of this book, I've aimed to share with you the parallels between golf and leadership and the enduring wisdom that both pursuits offer. Whether you're a golfer looking to improve your leadership skills or a leader seeking inspiration from golf, I hope you've found valuable insights that resonate with you.

Leadership, like golf, is a continuous journey. It's a path filled with challenges, opportunities for growth, and moments of reflection. As you continue your leadership journey, I encourage you to embrace the principles we've explored together—integrity, focus, strategic thinking, motivation, attention to detail, continuous improvement, resilience, patience, fairness, and the pursuit of a lasting legacy. These are the qualities that not only define exceptional leaders but also lead to a fulfilling and impactful life.

Working closely with someone like Tommy Jacobs taught me that greatness in any field—whether on the fairway or in the boardroom—is achieved through a commitment to these timeless principles. His example, both as a golfer and a man, reminds us that authentic leadership is about more than just success; it's about how we approach the game and the legacy we leave behind.

As you close this book, I hope you carry a renewed sense of purpose, a deeper appreciation for the parallels between golf and leadership, and a commitment to continuously strive for excellence in all you do. Remember, every round of golf and every day as a leader presents a new opportunity to learn, grow, and make a positive impact.

Thank you for walking this fairway with me. The journey doesn't end here—it's only just begun.

Wayne E. Smith August 15, 2024

Teeing Up Success

Further Leadership Lessons from Golf

Various books, articles, and talks have explored the parallels between golf and leadership. Here's a curated list that delves into this topic:

Books:

"Golf and the Game of Leadership: An 18-Hole Guide for Success in Business and Life" by Donald E. McHugh

This book draws analogies between the game of golf and leadership principles, presenting 18 "holes" or lessons that apply both on the course and in business.

"Leadership and Golf (Creating Organizational Alignment) SWING to BALANCE" by William J. White.

White uses golf as a metaphor to discuss organizational alignment and effective leadership strategies.

"FairWays to Leadership®: Building Your Business Network One Round of Golf at a Time" by Mackenzie Mack and Jennifer Hall

This guidebook emphasizes how golf can be a tool for developing leadership and networking skills in the business world.

"The Inner Game of Golf" by W. Timothy Gallwey

Gallwey explores the mental aspects of golf, offering insights that apply to personal and professional excellence.

Articles:

"The 'Links' Between Golf and Leadership" by John Kotter

This article, published in Forbes, discusses how lessons from golf can be applied to leadership, emphasizing strategic thinking and adaptability.

"How Playing Golf Helps My Leadership Journey at Work" by Leaderonomics.com

This piece explores the parallels between golf and leadership, highlighting how the sport teaches patience, strategic thinking, and resilience.

"Golf and Leadership: How the Psychology of the Game Builds Stronger Leaders" by Kaili Purviance

The article delves into how golf fosters essential leadership qualities such as focus, resilience, and strategic planning.

Talks:

"The Inner Game of Work" by W. Timothy Gallwey

In this talk, Gallwey extends his "Inner Game" concepts from sports to the workplace, discussing how principles from golf and tennis can enhance leadership and performance.

"Leadership Lessons from Golf" by Selion Global

This presentation highlights how the qualities that make champion golfers—strategic focus, resilience, and precision—can transform executives into visionary leaders.

"Golf as a Tool for Executive Leadership Development" by Dawnet Beverley

A study examines executives' golf experiences to identify what they have learned about leadership from the game.

These resources offer diverse perspectives on how the principles and experiences of golf can inform and enhance leadership skills.

The Honor Code: Pro Golfers Who Lead with Integrity.

Golf has long been celebrated as a sport emphasizing integrity, with players often acting as their own referees and upholding the game's honor. Here are some notable professional golfers who have exemplified this virtue through their actions:

Bobby Jones

At the 1925 U.S. Open, Bobby Jones faced a situation that tested his adherence to the rules. On the 11th hole, as he prepared to pitch onto the green, his club brushed the grass, causing a slight ball movement. Despite no one else noticing, Jones called a penalty on himself. This self-imposed penalty ultimately led to him losing the tournament by one stroke. When praised for his honesty, Jones remarked, "You might as well praise me for not robbing banks."

Brian Davis

In 2010, during a playoff at the Verizon Heritage tournament, Brian Davis inadvertently touched a loose reed in a hazard during his backswing. Aware that this constituted a rules violation, he immediately called a penalty on himself, resulting in the loss of the playoff. His act of integrity was widely praised in the golf community.

Annika Sörenstam

As an assistant captain during the 2015 Solheim Cup, Annika Sörenstam faced controversy when the U.S. team accused her of advising a European player, which was against the rules. Sörenstam vehemently denied the accusation, maintaining her commitment to the integrity of the game.

Billy Horschel

In September 2024, Billy Horschel narrowly defeated Rory McIlroy in a playoff to win the BMW PGA Championship at Wentworth. Despite the loss, McIlroy displayed exceptional sportsmanship by congratulating Horschel, showcasing the mutual respect and integrity prevalent among top golfers.

These instances highlight the deep-rooted culture of honesty and integrity in professional golf, where players often prioritize the spirit of the game over personal gain.

Beyond Power: Leaders Who Choose Integrity Over Influence

These leaders inspire trust and set ethical standards within their organizations and communities. Here are a few notable examples:

Warren Buffett

During the 2008 financial crisis, Warren Buffett invested $5 billion in Goldman Sachs, bolstering confidence in the banking sector and demonstrating his commitment to stability and ethical business practices.

Indra Nooyi

As CEO of PepsiCo, Indra Nooyi shifted the company's focus toward healthier products despite potential short-term profit losses, showcasing her dedication to integrity and long-term societal well-being.

Tim Cook

Apple CEO Tim Cook upheld user privacy by resisting FBI demands to unlock an iPhone, making ethical decisions prioritizing customer trust and data security.

Mahatma Gandhi

An anecdote highlighting Gandhi's integrity involves a mother seeking his advice to discourage her son's sugar consumption. Gandhi asked her to return in 30 days, during which he abstained from sugar, ensuring he led by example before advising others.

Jimmy Carter

The 39th U.S. President, Jimmy Carter, was renowned for his moral integrity and human rights advocacy. After his presidency, he founded the Carter Center, advancing democracy and combating disease globally. In 2002, he earned a Nobel Peace Prize.

Thuli Madonsela

As South Africa's Public Protector, Thuli Madonsela received the 2014 Transparency International Integrity Award for her unwavering commitment to truth and justice and for exemplifying ethical leadership.

Peter Eigen

The founder of Transparency International, Peter Eigen, has been recognized for his dedication to combating corruption and promoting transparency, earning prestigious awards for his efforts.

These leaders have demonstrated integrity by setting benchmarks for ethical conduct in various fields.

www.ingramcontent.com/pod-product-compliance
Lightning Source LLC
Chambersburg PA
CBHW071304040426
42444CB00009B/1860